MW00604104

Bright Kids™ Practice Test Three for the OLSAT® – Level E (Fourth and Fifth Grade)

Written and published by: Bright Kids Publications™

Bright Kids Publications™
225 Broadway
Suite 1400
New York, NY 10007

Phone: 917-539-4575
Email: info@brightkidsnyc.com
www.brightkidsnyc.com

Table of Contents

About Bright Kids NYC™

Bright Kids NYC™ was founded in New York City to provide language arts and math enrichment for young children. Our goal is to prepare students of all ages for standardized exams through assessments, tutoring, parent workshops, and our publications. Our philosophy is that, regardless of age, test taking is a skill that can be acquired and mastered through practice.

At Bright Kids NYC™, we strive to provide the best learning materials. Our publications are truly unique. All of our books have been created by qualified psychologists, learning specialists, teachers, and staff writers. Our books have also been tested by hundreds of children in our tutoring practice. Since children can make associations that many adults cannot, testing of materials by children is a critical step towards creating successful test preparation guides. Finally, our learning specialists, teaching staff, and writers have provided practical strategies and tips to help students compete successfully on standardized exams.

Feel free to contact us if you have any questions.

Corporate Headquarters
Bright Kids NYC™ Inc.
225 Broadway
Suite 1400
New York, NY 10007

Phone: 917-539-4575
Email: info@brightkidsnyc.com
www.brightkidsnyc.com

Bright Kids™ Practice Test Three for the OLSAT® – Level E (Fourth and Fifth Grade)

Introduction

Bright Kids NYC™ created the OLSAT® practice tests to familiarize students with the content and format of the OLSAT®. Students, no matter how bright they may be, do not always perform well if they are not accustomed to the format and structure of a standardized exam. They can misunderstand the directions or fail to carefully read a question and properly consider all of the answer choices. Thus, without adequate preparation and familiarization, a student may not perform to the best of his or her ability on a standardized exam like the OLSAT®.

The Bright Kids™ practice tests for the OLSAT® Level E can be used as diagnostic tools to help assess a student's ability to perform well on the various question types on the actual exam. If you have purchased our preparation guide for Levels D, E, and F, you can use the practice test in this book to see how well you may perform on a simulated OLSAT®.

The Bright Kids™ practice tests for the OLSAT® Level E are not designed to generate a score or a percentile rank since they have not been standardized with actual OLSAT® norms and standards. The objectives of the practice tests are to identify a student's strengths, weaknesses, and overall test-taking ability in order to adequately prepare him or her for the actual exam. Our answer key lists the question type for every test question in this book. You should use the answer key to easily identify the types of OLSAT® questions that you find difficult to solve.

In order to maximize the effectiveness of the Bright Kids™ practice tests for the OLSAT® Level E, it is important to first familiarize yourself with the test and its instructions. In addition, it is recommended that you take the practice tests in a neutral environment free of noise and clutter. Finally, a comfortable seating arrangement may help you focus and concentrate to the best of your ability.

Most students will have to take numerous standardized exams throughout their school years. The best way to develop the critical thinking skills for these types of exams is to practice with similarly-styled exams under test-like conditions. This method helps ensure that a student will succeed on his or her exam.

OLSAT® Overview

The *Otis-Lennon School Ability Test*® (OLSAT®) was created and published by Dr. Arthur Otis at Stanford University in 1918. The *Otis Group Intelligence Scale* was followed by the *Otis Self-Administering Tests of Mental Ability*, the *Otis Quick-Scoring Mental Ability Tests*, the *Otis-Lennon Mental Ability Test*, and finally the *Otis-Lennon School Ability Test*®. The purpose of the exam is to assess a student's aptitude for in-school performance by testing his or her cognitive and reasoning abilities.

The latest version of the *Otis-Lennon School Ability Test*® is the eighth edition (OLSAT® 8) and it is administered in various education programs in New York, Connecticut, California, Texas, and Virginia. Some of these programs are described below.

New York City Gifted and Talented programs administer the OLSAT® for entry into district and citywide Gifted and Talented programs. The OLSAT® is administered in connection with the *Naglieri Nonverbal Ability Test*®- *Second Edition* (NNAT®2). Currently, students are required to perform at or above the 90th percentile rank to be eligible for the district programs and at or above the 97th percentile to be eligible for the citywide programs. Additional information can be found at http://schools.nyc.gov/Academics/GiftedandTalented.

The Davis Unified School District in California uses the OLSAT® for students in Grades 3-8 to qualify for entry into the district Gifted and Talented programs. Students must receive a total OLSAT® score of 96% or higher and a Verbal or Nonverbal score in the 96th percentile or higher to qualify for the Gifted and Talented Education programs (GATE).

The Greenwich Public Schools District Board of Education uses the OLSAT® in conjunction with the *Stanford Achievement Test Series* to evaluate students in the third, fifth, and seventh grades. Each student's OLSAT® score helps predict his or her performance on the *Stanford Achievement Test Series* and enables the district to compare achievement scores. The OLSAT® is also used to predict performance on the *Connecticut Mastery Test*, a mandated year-end exam.

Content of the OLSAT® Level E Test (Fourth and Fifth Grade)

In order to succeed on the OLSAT®, students must accurately perceive pattern relationships and recall what has been perceived. Students also need to use their reasoning abilities to comprehend abstract items and apply generalizations to new and different contexts. These reasoning abilities are measured through the student's performance on verbal and nonverbal questions.

Verbal Questions

The verbal questions are divided into two types: verbal comprehension and verbal reasoning. **Verbal comprehension** questions are designed to measure the student's ability to extrapolate and manipulate information from language. These questions emphasize the relational aspects of words, sentences, and their nuances of meaning.

1) **Antonyms:** Antonym questions require the student to identify the opposite meaning of a word. Antonym questions mainly test a student's vocabulary skills; however, a student must also possess a comprehensive definition of the word in order to reverse its meaning and identify the correct answer choice.

2) **Sentence Completion:** These questions assess a student's ability to make the necessary logical connections involved in sentence composition. He or she will have to "fill in the blank(s)" with the missing word(s) necessary to best complete the sentence.

3) **Sentence Arrangement:** These types of questions take the form of a sentence jumble. A student must look at the random assortment of words and determine the best possible order they can form to make a meaningful sentence.

Verbal reasoning questions are designed to measure the student's ability to identify patterns and relationships between words.and sentences. A student will have to use his or her vocabulary and deductive reasoning skills to solve a number of different types of questions that test his or her verbal reasoning abilities.

1) **Arithmetic Reasoning:** Arithmetic reasoning incorporates mathematical reasoning into the solving of verbal problems. This section tests basic mathematical concepts like the addition, subtraction, multiplication, and division of whole numbers, fractions, or decimals.

2) **Logical Selection:** These questions ask a student to apply logic in order to find the necessary answer, or the answer that is true in every possible instance, to complete a short statement. These questions require a level of focused reasoning since the student must differentiate between the answers that *could* be correct versus the answer that is *always* correct.

3) **Word/Letter Matrix:** These questions require a student to determine the relationship between the words or letters in a matrix in order to identify the missing letter or word that belongs in the matrix.

4) **Verbal Analogies:** An analogy is defined as a similarity between two things on which a comparison may be based. Analogy questions require a student to infer a relationship between the first two items and then select an item that completes the second relationship in the same manner. For verbal analogy questions on the OLSAT®, a student will need to find the relationship between the first pair of words given to him or her. Then, he or she must apply the same relationship to a different word in order to identify the correct answer choice.

5) **Verbal Classifications:** Verbal classification questions require a student to find the one word that doesn't belong among a given set of answer choices. In order to find the correct answer, he or she will have to identify a characteristic that exists among four of the five words. The word that doesn't share the same characteristic as the other four words is the correct answer.

6) **Inference:** Inference questions require a student to identify a conclusion that is never explicitly stated but can be logically deduced from the information given in the question. These questions test a student's ability to evaluate the premises and differentiate between necessary and possible conclusions.

Nonverbal Questions

The nonverbal questions are divided into two types: figural and quantitative reasoning. Figural reasoning questions are designed to measure a student's ability to reason through a visual, or non-language based, medium. For these types of questions, a student must be able to infer relationships, determine the next step(s) in an identifiable sequence, and make generalizations from recognizable figural patterns.

1) **Figural Analogy:** Analogical reasoning is the ability to use parallel cases to draw a conclusion. For students, analogical reasoning on the OLSAT® is assessed through verbal or figural elements. For figural analogy questions on the OLSAT®, a student will have to identify the relationship between a pair of figures and then complete a second pair using the same relationship.

2) **Pattern Matrix:** Pattern matrix questions evaluate a student's ability to find the next step in a geometric series based on a set of rules. A student will need to identify and apply the rule to determine the shape that belongs in place of the question mark in the matrix.

3) **Figural Series:** Figural series questions assess the student's skill at evaluating a sequential series of geometric shapes and then predicting the next geometric figure in the sequence.

The **quantitative reasoning** questions measure a student's ability to infer patterns, relationships, and to solve problems utilizing numbers instead of language. In order to correctly answer these questions, a student must predict and establish outcomes based on mathematical processes.

1) **Number Series:** Similar to the figure series questions, a student will need to extrapolate a pattern from a sequence of numbers and then apply that pattern to predict what will come next in the series of numbers.

2) **Numeric Inference:** Numeric inference questions require a student to discover the relationship between different pairs or trios of numbers in order to find the number that belongs in place of the question mark. Students will need to use their arithmetic reasoning and computational skills to determine the rule that governs the sets of numbers in the boxes in the question.

3) **Number Matrix:** Number matrix questions test a student's ability to find an overarching principle that links the numbers in a matrix in order to determine what number is missing from the matrix.

OLSAT® Level E Structure

The OLSAT® is a multiple-choice test. Reading skills are an important component of the Level E test since students will need to complete every question on their own in a timed situation. The OLSAT® Level E test is administered in a group setting and students are required to mark or bubble in their answers. The content and structure of the OLSAT® varies for each grade level. The Level E test is given to fourth and fifth grade students and contains 72 questions that test a student's verbal and nonverbal reasoning skills. Students are given 40 minutes to complete the test.

TABLE 1: Distribution of Types of Questions[1]

Types of Questions	Number of Questions
VERBAL	**36**
Verbal Comprehension	
Antonyms	4
Sentence Completion	4
Sentence Arrangement	4
Verbal Reasoning	
Arithmetic Reasoning	4
Logical Selection	4
Word/Letter Matrix	4
Verbal Analogies	4
Verbal Classification	4
Inference	4
NONVERBAL	**36**
Figural Reasoning	
Figural Analogies	6
Pattern Matrix	6
Figural Series	6
Quantitative Reasoning	
Number Series	6
Numeric Inference	6
Number Matrix	6
Total	**72**

[1] This chart may not reflect the exact distribution of questions on the actual exam since the mix between verbal and nonverbal questions and among different types of questions varies from year to year.

Scoring Guidelines

The results of the OLSAT® comprise a wealth of useful information for test users. Derived scores based on age and grade comparisons can be provided for verbal, nonverbal, and total raw scores. Raw scores, which are defined as the number of questions answered correctly, do not provide enough information about the quality of students' performances. However, a scaled score system connects all test levels and yields a continuous scale that can be used to compare the performances of students taking different levels of the same content cluster. Scaled scores are particularly useful for evaluating changes in performance over time and for out-of-level testing. Scaled scores can also be translated into percentile ranks. For example, New York City Gifted and Talented programs only provide percentile ranks and composite scores while other districts in the United States provide more detailed information.

Since the test changes from year to year, the number of questions a student can answer correctly to obtain a specific scaled score will vary based on that particular test's curve and distribution. OLSAT® scores also take into account the age of the student. The test is normed in three-month age bands; students who are younger can miss more questions and still get the same percentile rank and scaled score as older students who are within the same grade.

The Bright Kids™ practice tests for the OLSAT® Level E can only be scored by the total number of correct answers. Please realize that a student can miss many questions on the actual test and still obtain a high score. Since this practice test has not been standardized with the OLSAT®, scaled scores or percentile ranks cannot be obtained from the raw score. Thus, the Bright Kids™ practice tests for the OLSAT® Level E should be utilized as a learning tool to help evaluate a student's strengths or weaknesses on various question types rather than to predict what his or her scaled score or percentile rank will be on the actual exam.

General Administration Guidelines

The Level E test is typically administered over the course of an hour. Students will need around 10 minutes to fill out their personal identification information on the answer document and test booklet. Then, the proctor will need approximately 10 minutes to administer five sample questions in order to familiarize students with the various question types on the test. Afterwards, students will begin the exam and have 40 minutes to complete as many of the 72 questions as possible. The recommended timeline for the following practice test is:

Examples   Approximately 10 minutes

Test Administration   40 minutes

Getting Ready

Materials

1)   The answer sheet, located in the back of this book

2)   Several No. 2 soft lead pencils, erasers, and pencil sharpeners

3)   Ideally, a "Do Not Disturb" sign for the room where the test will be administered

Prior to Testing

1)   Familiarize yourself with the test and its instructions.

2)   Make sure there is ample lighting and ventilation in the room where the test will be administered.

3)   To prevent interruptions, the student should take the test where there will be no distractions. If the house is not suitable, try to find a local library or school.

During Testing

1)   Make sure that the student is comfortable marking down the answers.

2)   Read all of the instructions exactly as they are written; do not paraphrase or change the questions.

3)   Adhere to the timing guidelines. The student should only be given 40 minutes to complete the entire test.

4)   Do not give the student any feedback during testing. Discuss the answers only after the completion of the test.

Bright Kids™ Practice Test for the OLSAT®

Instructions and Sample Questions

Level E

Fourth and Fifth Grade

Test Three

Instructions

You should sit down with the student before administering the practice test and go over the following sample questions with him or her. The script on the left-hand pages gives instructions on what to say for each sample question. The script has been bolded to help differentiate it from the rest of the directions. After the administration of Sample Questions A through E, the student must finish the practice test on his or her own.

Sample Questions and Test Administration

SAY: **Today, you are going to answer some questions in this book.**

SAMPLE A

SAY: **Look at Sample A and read the problem to yourself. Then, mark down your answer in the "Sample Questions" box on the row labeled "A" on your answer sheet.**

Pause while the student reads and answers the question.

SAY: **In this question, the first two figures go together in a certain way. There is a horizontal line in both shapes. Also, the black triangle has switched sides from one shape to the next. Which figure among the answer choices goes with the third figure in the same way? The correct figure will be a square with a black circle to the right of a vertical line. That figure can be seen in answer choice (D), so it is the correct answer. You should have filled in the bubble labeled "D" on your answer sheet.**

Make sure the student is comfortable with the answer to Sample A before proceeding.

SAMPLE B

SAY: **Now look at Sample B and read the problem to yourself. Then, mark down your answer in the "Sample Questions" box on the row labeled "B" on your answer sheet.**

Pause while the student reads and answers the question.

SAY: **In this question, there is a number missing in the number series. What number belongs in place of the question mark? The first number is 14, the next number is 17, the third number is 20, and the fourth number is 23. The pattern is to add 3 to the previous number in order to get the next number in the series. The number that belongs in place of the question mark is 26. Thus, the correct answer is choice (C). You should have filled in the bubble labeled "C" on your answer sheet.**

Make sure the student is comfortable with the answer to Sample B before proceeding.

Sample Questions

A.

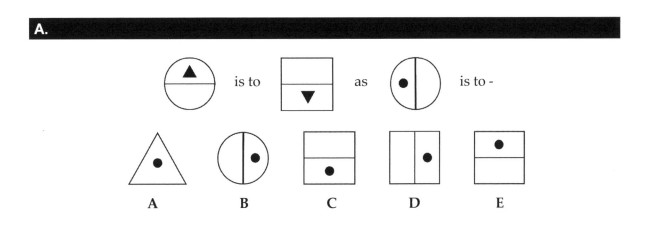

B.

What number is missing in this series?

14 17 20 23 **?**

A. 24   **B.** 25   **C.** 26   **D.** 27   **E.** 28

SAMPLE C

SAY: **Now look at Sample C and read the problem to yourself. Then, mark down your answer in the "Sample Questions" box on the row labeled "C" on your answer sheet.**

Pause while the student reads and answers the question.

SAY: **In this question, the first two words go together in a certain way. A shoe can be put on a foot. What can be put on a hand? The correct answer is choice (B); a glove can be put on a hand. A shoe goes on a foot like a glove goes on a hand, so answer choice (B) is correct. You should have filled in the bubble labeled "B" on your answer sheet.**

Make sure the student is comfortable with the answer to Sample C before proceeding.

SAMPLE D

SAY: **Now look at Sample D and read the problem to yourself. Then, mark down your answer in the "Sample Questions" box on the row labeled "D" on your answer sheet.**

Pause while the student reads and answers the question.

SAY: **In this question, the drawings in the row go together in a certain way. What drawing belongs in place of the question mark? The figure is rotating 90 degrees in a clockwise direction and the circle is alternating between black and white in each new drawing. The drawing that belongs in place of the question mark is a white circle with a downwards pointing arrow. Thus, the correct answer is choice (A). You should have filled in the bubble labeled "A" on your answer sheet.**

Make sure the student is comfortable with the answer to Sample D before proceeding.

C.

Foot is to **shoe**, as **hand** is to:

A. scarf   B. glove   C. sweater   D. pants   E. earring

D.

The drawings below form a series. Which drawing continues that series and goes where you see the question mark?

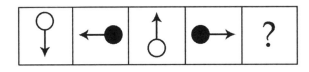

                    A   B   C   D   E

SAMPLE E

SAY: **Now look at Sample E and read the problem to yourself. Then, mark down your answer in the "Sample Questions" box on the row labeled "E" on your answer sheet.**

Pause while the student reads and answers the question.

SAY: **In this question, the words in the box go together in a certain way. Which word belongs in place of the question mark? The second word in each row has added a letter to the beginning of the first word in the row. In the first row, the third word has added a letter to the end of the second word. Thus, the third word in the second row should have added one letter to the end of the word "bit". The only word among the answer choices that has added one letter to the end of the word "bit" is "bite". Thus, the correct answer is choice (E). You should have filled in the bubble labeled "E" on your answer sheet.**

Make sure the student is comfortable with the answer to Sample E before proceeding.

SAY: **The problems on the following pages are similar to the sample problems you just solved. Read each question carefully and choose the best answer. Make sure that you mark all of your answers down on the correct line of your answer sheet. You will have 40 minutes to complete this test. If you are having trouble with a question, skip it and go on to the next question. You may not have time to answer every question, but try to answer as many as you can. If you make it to where the word "STOP" is printed at the bottom of the page, you may check your work until time is called. Do you have any questions?**

Answer any questions the student may have before proceeding.

SAY: **Now you may begin working.**

Make sure that you start timing as the student begins reading the questions on the following pages. At the end of 40 minutes, the student must stop working on the practice test.

E.

The words in the box go together in a certain way. Which word goes where you see the question mark?

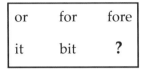

or	for	fore
it	bit	?

A. bitten   **B.** bate   **C.** blink   **D.** bitter   **E.** bite

Bright Kids™ Practice Test for the OLSAT®

Student's Booklet

Level E

Fourth and Fifth Grade

Test Three

01

The opposite of **sever** is -

A unite   B undo   C discover   D apply   E slither

02

Choose the words that **best** complete the sentence below.

Don't _____ on the _____ meeting.

A invade - public
B infringe - delicious
C withdraw - important
D object - intelligent
E intrude - private

03

If the words below were arranged to make the **best** sentence, what would be the beginning letter of the **last** word in the sentence?

the	get	wrong	don't	on	bus

A t   B g   C w   D d   E b

04

What number is one-fifth the sum of fifteen and twenty?

A 5   B 7   C 8   D 10   E 15

05 Daniel, Brian, Hannah, and Chad are all standing in line. Brian is behind Hannah who is before Chad but behind Daniel. We know for certain that -

A Chad is in front of Brian
B Hannah likes movie theaters
C Daniel is in front of Brian, Hannah, and Chad
D Hannah is behind Brian
E Chad and Brian are standing side by side

06 The words in the box go together in a certain way. Choose the word that goes where you see the question mark.

flour	sour	our
?	pout	out

A flower   B outer   C mount   D trout   E devour

07 **Vehicle** is to **car** as -

A dolphin is to whale
B toe is to shoe
C liquid is to milk
D cheese is to mouse
E angry is to frustrated

08 Which word does **not** belong with the other four words?

A poverty   B deficiency   C scarcity   D hardship   E prosperity

09

A professor cannot teach without -

A books
B students
C a desk
D a classroom
E essays

10

The drawings in the box go together in a certain way. Choose the drawing that goes where you see the question mark.

is to   as   is to -

    A   B   C   D   E

11

The drawings in the box go together in a certain way. Choose the drawing that goes where you see the question mark.

?

    A   B   C   D   E

12

The drawings below form a series. Which drawing continues that series and goes where you see the question mark?

?

    A   B   C   D   E

13 What number is missing in this series?

14   12   13   11   12   10   11   9   **?**

A 9   B 10   C 11   D 12   E 13

14 The numbers in each box go together following the **same** rule. Figure out the rule and then choose the number that goes where you see the question mark.

13, 26   22, 44   55, **?**

A 26   B 44   C 66   D 82   E 110

15 The numbers in the box go together in a certain way. Choose the number that goes where you see the question mark.

1	4	7
33	36	?
92	95	98

A 37   B 38   C 39   D 42   E 47

16

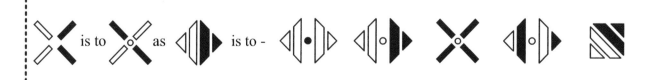

A   B   C   D   E

17 The drawings below form a series. Which drawing continues that series and goes where you see the question mark?

A	B	C	D	E

18 The numbers in each box go together following the same rule. Figure out the rule and then choose the number that goes where you see the question mark.

9, 3	21, **?**	33, 27

A 7   B 12   C 14   D 15   E 21

19 The opposite of **immense** is -

A vast   B frigid   C calm   D tiny   E incomplete

20 Choose the words that best complete the sentence below.

Everyone _____ the fire truck driving down the street because the siren was so _____.

A saw - quiet
B felt - interesting
C heard - shrill
D ran to - subtle
E perceived - capable

21 If the words below were arranged to make the **best** sentence, what would be the beginning letter of the **last** word in the sentence?

on   summer   your   have   fun   vacation

A f   B v   C o   D s   E h

22 What number is twice the difference between nineteen and seven?

A 24   B 20   C 18   D 17   E 12

23 Hazel got more ice cream scoops than Kenneth and Zeke but fewer scoops than Lina. Pedro didn't get any ice cream. We know for certain that -

A Lina got the most ice cream scoops
B Kenneth didn't get ice cream
C Zeke got as many scoops as Kenneth
D Pedro doesn't like ice cream
E Lina got fewer scoops than Zeke

24 The words in the box go together in a certain way. Which word goes where you see the question mark?

hop	hope	open
no	now	?

A owl   B towel   C nose   D opened   E happen

25

Cease is to **stop** as **start** is to -

A temper B defeat C repeal D commence E approach

26

Which word does not belong with the other four words?

A intellect B wisdom C ignorance D brilliance E genius

27

There can be no novels without -

A bindings B titles C chapters D writers E computers

28

is to ▢ as △ is to -   ◯ ▢ ◇ ◇ △

A B C D E

29 The drawings in the box go together in a certain way. Which drawing goes where you see the question mark?

30 The drawings below form a series. Which drawing continues that series and goes where you see the question mark?

31 What number is missing in this series?

2   6   14   30   62   **?**

A 62   B 64   C 100   D 120   E 126

32 The numbers in each box go together by following the same rule. Figure out the rule and then choose the number that goes where you see the question mark.

| 10, 35, 30 | 16, **?**, 36 | 22, 47, 42 |

A 16   B 27   C 31   D 32   E 41

33 The numbers in the box go together in a certain way. Choose the number that goes where you see the question mark.

80	36	14
40	16	4
60	?	9

A 18   B 20   C 24   D 26   E 40

---

34 The opposite of **feeble** is -

A weak   B tempting   C sturdy   D lazy   E anxious

---

35 The drawings in the box go together in a certain way. Which drawing goes where you see the question mark?

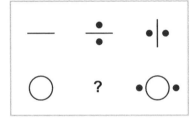

A   B   C   D   E

---

36 What comes next in the series?

3   4   Z   6   7   Y   9   10   X   ?

A 12   B 13   C 14   D 15   E 16

37

Choose the words that best complete the sentence below.

She _____ to eat the corned beef _____ she was hungry.

A wanted - although
B hurried - nevertheless
C hustled - except
D refused - although
E resolved - even if

38

The numbers in the box go together in a certain way. Which number goes where you see the question mark?

17,17	20,14	23,11
10,20	13,17	?

A 16, 14   B 17, 13   C 20, 20   D 12, 24   E 15, 27

39

The numbers in each box go together following the same rule. Figure out the rule and then choose the number that goes where you see the question mark.

| 41, 45, 53 | | 74, 78, 86 | | 67, 71, **?** |

A 71   B 79   C 81   D 83   E 85

40

♥ is to ⟨symbols⟩ as ☆ is to -

A   B   C   D   E

41 Every fruit has -

A seeds   B pits   C stems   D leaves   E rinds

42 The drawings in the box go together in a certain way. Which drawing goes where you see the question mark.

            A   B   C   D   E

43 What number is missing in this series?

2   2   4   12   48   **?**

A 200   B 220   C 240   D 260   E 268

44 If the words below were arranged to make the **best** sentence, what would be the beginning letter of the **first** word in the sentence?

| the | while | hot | eat | it's | soup |

A w   B e   C h   D s   E t

45 There are three times as many elephants as there are bears at the zoo. If there are sixteen elephants and bears in total, how many bears are at the zoo?

A 16   B 12   C 10   D 8   E 4

46 Last week, Nicole went to the mall on Tuesday and Thursday. Sheryl went to the mall every day of the week except for Monday, Friday, and Saturday. Suzanne never went to the mall on the same day that Nicole or Sheryl went to the mall. We know for certain that -

A Nicole went to the mall on Monday.
B Suzanne went to the mall on Wednesday.
C Sheryl likes going to the mall more than Nicole likes going to the mall.
D Both Sheryl and Nicole went to the mall on Tuesday and Thursday.
E Both Suzanne and Sheryl went to the mall on Friday.

47 The drawings below form a series. Which drawing continues that series and goes where you see the question mark?

A   B   C   D   E

48 The numbers in each box go together following the same rule. Figure out that rule and then choose the number that goes where you see the question mark.

| 60, 20 | 30, 10 | **?**, 12 |

A 14   B 18   C 30   D 36   E 48

49

The opposite of **hasty** is -

A quick   B sluggish   C wasteful   D tardy   E content

50

 is to as is to -

A   B   C   D   E

51

What number is missing in this series?

11   12   14   17   23   35   59   **?**

A 100   B 103   C 107   D 118   E 125

52

The drawings in the box go together in a certain way. Choose the drawing that goes where you see the question mark.

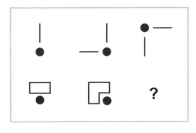

A   B   C   D   E

53 The numbers in the box go together in a certain way. Which number goes where you see the question mark?

3, 4	7, 8	15, 16
6, 8	14, 16	?

A 15, 16   B 16, 18   C 20, 21   D 24, 26   E 30, 32

54 Choose the words that best complete the sentence below.

Cooking was _____ for him, so he decided to become a _____.

A effortless - chef
B simple - father
C surprising - cook
D haphazard - restaurant owner
E straightforward - fireman

55 **Avoid** is to **approach** as **destroy** is to -

A build   B suspend   C hoist   D fade   E tower

56

is to [triangle figure] as [flower figure] is to -

A   B   C   D   E

57

What number is missing in this series?

48   50   45   47   42   44   **?**   41

A 30   B 32   C 35   D 39   E 42

58

If the words below were arranged to make the **best** sentence, what would be the beginning letter of the **first** word in the sentence?

| storm | found | the | during | refuge | he |

A h   B d   C r   D f   E s

59

The numbers in the box go together in a certain way. Choose the number that goes where you see the question mark.

21	22	24
27	34	48
31	42	64
28	36	**?**

A 24   B 36   C 44   D 48   E 52

60

The drawings below form a series. Which drawing continues that series and goes where you see the question mark?

A   B   C   D   E

61

Which word does **not** belong with the other four words?

A French   B Asian   C African   D European   E Australian

62

The words in the box go together in a certain way. Choose the word that goes where you see the question mark.

tend	?	trend
sand	and	stand

A and   B fend   C end   D send   E ten

63

The drawings below form a series. Which drawing continues that series and goes where you see the question mark?

A   B   C   D   E

64

Moveable is to **object** as **navigable** is to -

A phone   B shoe   C statue   D ruler   E ship

65

The numbers in the box go together in a certain way. Choose the number that goes where you see the question mark.

3	?	23
11	21	31

A 33   B 23   C 21   D 13   E 11

66

There are half as many apples as oranges in a basket. If there are thirty fruits in the basket, how many of them are oranges?

A 10   B 15   C 20   D 22   E 30

67

The drawings in the box go together in a certain way. Which drawing goes where you see the question mark.

A   B   C   D   E

68

Hope has three more lollipops than Diedra and five less than Xander. Vincent has more lollipops than Alex, who has five more lollipops than Xander and ten more than Hope. We know for certain that -

A   Diedra has the least amount of lollipops.
B   Alex has fifteen lollipops.
C   Xander has more lollipops than Vincent.
D   Xander had fewer lollipops than Diedra.
E   Hope has as many lollipops as Xander.

69 The words in the box go together in a certain way. Choose the word that goes where you see the question mark.

triple	ripple	rip
dearer	**?**	ear

A reader   B earner   C dare   D earmark   E clearer

---

70 Which word does **not** belong with the other four words?

A octagon   B hexagon   C cube   D triangle   E square

---

71 There can be no police officers without -

A badges   B uniforms   C laws   D sirens   E handcuffs

---

72 The numbers in each box go together following the same rule. Figure out that rule and then choose the number that goes where you see the question mark.

81, 9	90, 10	9, ?

A 1   B 2   C 3   D 4   E 5

Answer Key

Answer Key

	Correct Answer	Student's Answer	Type of Question
1.	A		Antonym
2.	E		Sentence Completion
3.	E		Sentence Arrangement
4.	B		Arithmetic Reasoning
5.	C		Inference
6.	D		Word/Letter Matrix
7.	C		Verbal Analogy
8.	E		Verbal Classification
9.	B		Logical Selection
10.	B		Figural Analogy
11.	C		Pattern Matrix
12.	E		Figural Series
13.	B		Number Series
14.	E		Numeric Inference
15.	C		Number Matrix
16.	D		Figural Analogy
17.	B		Figural Series
18.	D		Numeric Inference
19.	D		Antonym
20.	C		Sentence Completion
21.	B		Sentence Arrangement
22.	A		Arithmetic Reasoning
23.	A		Inference
24.	A		Word/Letter Matrix
25.	D		Verbal Analogy

Answer Key (Continued)

	Correct Answer	Student's Answer	Type of Question
26.	C		Verbal Classification
27.	D		Logical Selection
28.	E		Figural Analogy
29.	B		Pattern Matrix
30.	A		Figural Series
31.	E		Number Series
32.	E		Numeric Inference
33.	D		Number Matrix
34.	C		Antonym
35.	D		Pattern Matrix
36.	A		Number Series
37.	D		Sentence Completion
38.	A		Number Matrix
39.	B		Numeric Inference
40.	C		Figural Analogy
41.	A		Logical Selection
42.	A		Pattern Matrix
43.	C		Number Series
44.	B		Sentence Arrangement
45.	E		Arithmetic Reasoning
46.	D		Inference
47.	D		Figural Series
48.	D		Numeric Inference
49.	B		Antonym
50.	B		Figural Analogy

Answer Key (Continued)

	Correct Answer	Student's Answer	Type of Question
51.	C		Number Series
52.	B		Pattern Matrix
53.	E		Number Matrix
54.	A		Sentence Completion
55.	A		Verbal Analogy
56.	E		Figural Analogy
57.	D		Number Series
58.	A		Sentence Arrangement
59.	E		Number Matrix
60.	C		Figural Series
61.	A		Verbal Classification
62.	C		Word/Letter Matrix
63.	B		Figural Series
64.	E		Verbal Analogy
65.	D		Number Matrix
66.	C		Arithmetic Reasoning
67.	B		Pattern Matrix
68.	A		Inference
69.	B		Word/Letter Matrix
70.	C		Verbal Classification
71.	C		Logical Selection
72.	A		Numeric Inference

Bright Kids™ Practice Test Three for the OLSAT® – Level E (Fourth and Fifth Grade)

Answer Explanations

Answer Explanations

1. Correct Answer: A

This antonym question asks you to determine which of the words in the answer choices means the opposite of the word in question. To sever is to cut, divide, or separate something. Thus, you are looking for a word that describes bringing things together. To "undo" (choice B) something is to unfasten something or to reverse an action. If you "discover" (choice C) something it means that you have found something new. "Apply" (choice D) is a good example of a word that might seem to be appropriate, but does not carry the exact opposite meaning of the word in question. To apply something is to make use of something or to put something into contact. Answer choice (D) is incorrect. To "slither" (choice E) is to slide along a surface from side to side or to move in a slippery manner, thus (E) is also incorrect. To unite is to combine or connect things. The word "unite" carries the exact opposite meaning of the word "sever". The best answer choice available is the word **(A) unite**.

2. Correct Answer: E

This sentence completion question requires you to insert the best pair of words that completes the sentence. In order for an answer choice to be correct, both words must make sense in the sentence. The best way to identify the correct answer is to insert the words from each answer choice into the sentence to see what makes the most sense. Should the sentence say, "Don't invade on the public meeting"? This may sound like it could be correct, but not quite. To "invade" is to enter someplace forcefully or to go in with the intent to take possession of something. It doesn't seem necessary to forcefully enter a public meeting with the intent to take it over, so answer choice (A) is incorrect. Could the sentence read, "Don't infringe on the delicious meeting"? How about, "Don't withdraw on the important meeting"? Neither of these sentences makes sense. "Delicious" is not an appropriate word to use to describe a meeting. Similarly, the phrase "withdraw on" does not make sense in the sentence. Answer choices (B) and (C) can be eliminated. Could the correct sentence read, "Don't object on the intelligent meeting"? The word "object" isn't being used properly in this sentence. You don't object "on" something; rather, you object "to" something. Answer choice (D) is incorrect. The sentence should read, "Don't intrude on the private meeting." To intrude is to interrupt or to enter without an invitation. The words "intrude" and "private" work together in this sentence because it makes sense to say that you shouldn't interrupt a meeting to which you are not invited. **Answer choice (E) is correct.**

3. **Correct Answer: E**

Here, this sentence arrangement question asks you to arrange a set of words in order to create the best possible sentence. Then, you must identify the first letter of the last word in the assembled sentence. The given words are, "the", "get", "wrong", "don't", "on", and "bus". Given this set of words, it makes the most sense to begin the sentence with the word "don't" as if it is the beginning of a command statement. Following that, the only verb in the sentence to pair with "don't" is "get", bringing you to "don't get". From the remaining words, you are left with "bus", a noun that can be modified by the adjective "wrong". Adding in the remaining word, "the", you arrive at the sentence, "Don't get on the wrong bus." The first letter of the last word in the sentence is **"b"**, so **answer choice (E)** is correct.

4. **Correct Answer: B**

This is an arithmetic reasoning question asking you to determine what number is one fifth the sum of fifteen and twenty. In order to answer this question correctly, you must first realize that the word "sum" means that the numbers fifteen and twenty are being added together. Based on the way the sentence is structured, you know that you must find the sum before you can do anything else. Once you arrive at the correct sum by solving for the equation $15 + 20$, which equals 35, the question directs you to identify the number that represents one-fifth of the sum. In order to arrive at the correct answer you must divide thirty-five through the equation $35 \div 5 = 7$. Thus, the correct answer is **(B) 7**.

5. ## Correct Answer: C

This inference question requires the use of logic in order to determine the correct answer. Here, you must carefully read a short statement in order to determine the correct order of people standing in line. For these types of questions, it is helpful to write out the order on a piece of scratch paper as you read the statement. The first sentence states that four people, Daniel, Brian, Hannah, and Chad, are standing in line. The next sentence states that Brian is behind Hannah who is before Chad but behind Daniel. Based on this information, what do we know for certain? Answer choice (B) can be eliminated immediately because movie theaters are not mentioned anywhere in the statement, so we cannot determine whether or not Hannah likes movie theaters. Answer choice (D), "Hannah is behind Brian", can be eliminated by looking at the original statement and noting that it directly states that Brian is behind Hannah. Answer choices (A) and (E) go together in that they pose alternative theories as to the positions of Brian and Chad. So, is Chad in front of Brian or are they standing side by side? We know that both Brian and Chad are standing behind Hannah and Daniel, but there is no information in the original statement that tells us Brian and Chad's position relative to each other in line. Since both answers could be correct, we do not know that either one is certain. Answers (A) and (E) are incorrect. The correct answer is **(C) "Daniel is in front of Brian, Hannah, and Chad."** If both Chad and Brian are standing behind Hannah and Hannah is standing behind Daniel, then Daniel must be standing in front of Brian, Hannah, and Chad.

6. ## Correct Answer: D

In this question, you are presented with a word matrix. In order to determine the correct answer, you must look at the words in the first row and identify what is happening to each word in order to create the last word in the row. Then you must apply the same pattern to the words in the second row and determine which word belongs in place of the question mark. The words in the first row are "flour", "sour", and "our". At first glance, you can see that all of the words share the last three letters. The second word is one letter shorter than the first, and the third word is one letter shorter than the second. In other words, as you go across the row from right to left, you add one letter, keeping only the last three the same. The words in the second row, reading from right to left, are "out" and "pout". Going by the rule for the first row, you should now look at the answer choices to find a five-letter word ending in "out". The correct answer is **(D) trout**.

7. Correct Answer: C

This is a verbal analogy question. Here, you must figure out the relationship between the pair of words in question and choose from among the answer choices the pair of words that are related in the same way. The first pair of words is "vehicle" and "car". A car is a type of vehicle. So, which of the pairs of words in the answer choices has the same relationship? Both dolphins and whales are mammals, but a whale is not a type of dolphin, so answer choice (A) is incorrect. A shoe is not a type of toe and a mouse is not a type of cheese, so answer choices (B) and (D) are incorrect. "Confused" and "angry" are both types of emotions, but being confused is not the same as being angry, so answer choice (E) is incorrect. The correct answer is **(C) "liquid is to milk"**, because milk is a type of liquid.

8. Correct Answer: E

For this verbal classification question, you must look at the words in the answer choices and identify which word is different than the others for one reason or another. The words presented in the answer choices are: "poverty" (choice A), "deficiency" (choice B), "scarcity" (choice C), "hardship" (choice D), and "prosperity" (choice E). So which one does not belong with the others? "Poverty", "deficiency", "scarcity", and "hardship" are all words that describe having a lack of something or relate to the concept of financial distress. "Prosperity" carries the opposite meaning and refers to financial success. Thus, the odd word out is **(E) prosperity**.

9. Correct Answer: B

This is your first logical selection question. Logical selection questions ask you to identify something that is always associated with a particular thing or concept. Here, you are asked to identify something that is always associated with a professor's ability to teach. Can a professor teach without "books" (choice A)? A lot of professors use books when teaching, but some classes, like performance or art classes, do not always require books. Answer choice (A) can be eliminated. Can a professor teach without "a desk" (choice C)? In many college classes, professors teach in large lecture halls without any desks in them. Additionally, a desk does not influence a person's ability to teach in any way, so answer choice (C) can also be eliminated. Can a professor teach without "a classroom" (choice D)? The ability to teach is not dependent on any particular location. People can teach over the internet, in someone's living room, or outside. Answer choice (D) is incorrect. Can a professor teach without "essays" (choice E)? Subjects like math, chemistry, and engineering often do not require the writing of essays. Can a professor teach without "students" (choice B)? Teaching is defined as imparting knowledge to someone else who is in turn a student. You cannot teach without having someone to teach to. **Answer choice (B) is correct.**

10. Correct Answer: B

Figural analogies are similar to verbal analogy questions and can be approached in much the same way. In this case, you must first figure out the relationship between the pair of figures in question and choose a pair from among the answer choices that is related in the same way. So, what was done to the first figure in order to get the second? The first shape in the pair is a white hexagon surrounding a smaller black square. The second picture shows a larger black square with four white circles attached to its corners. The relationship seems to be that the smaller shape in the center grows bigger, and the outer shape is removed and replaced with small circles attached at the corners. In the second pair of figures, you see a small, black triangle surrounded by a larger white square. Following the same rule as with the previous pair, the next shape should be a large black triangle with three white circles attached to its corners. **Answer choice (B)** is correct.

11. Correct Answer: C

This pattern matrix question can be approached in the same way you approach a word matrix. In order to determine the correct answer, you must look at the figures in the top row of the matrix and identify what is happening to each figure in order to create the last figure in the row. Then, apply the same pattern to the figures in the second row in order to determine which figure belongs in place of the question mark. Moving from left to right at the top row, you first see a white circle with a small black circle hovering outside it at the top right. Then, you see the same figure with an added small, black circle hovering off its left side. The third figure takes the previous figure and adds another small, black circle hovering at the white circle's bottom right. The rule appears to be that in every new figure, a small, black circle has been added in a triangular pattern in relation to the other black circles. The bottom row shows the same progression of black circles being added to each figure, but instead of a white circle at the center there is a white square. The third shape is missing, replaced by a question mark. Following the same pattern as in the top row, you are looking for a white square with a small, black circle hovering outside the top right, the left, and the bottom right of the white square in relation to each other. **Answer choice (C)** is correct.

12. Correct Answer: E

Here you are presented with a series of figures that change according to a specific pattern. The last figure in the series has been replaced with a question mark, and you must determine which figure in the answer choices belongs in place of the question mark. So, what is happening to each figure as you view the figures from left to right? The first figure is a black arrow pointing straight up. The second figure is a white triangle surrounding a black arrow that is pointing to the right. The next figure is a white square surrounding a black arrow pointing straight down. The fourth figure is a white pentagon with a black arrow pointing to the left. Two things appear to be changing in each figure. First, the shapes surrounding the arrows, once they appear, seem to increase by one side for each new figure in the series, so you go from a triangle with three sides to a square with four sides to a pentagon with five sides. Second, the black arrow at the center of each figure appears to be rotated 90 degrees clockwise in each new figure. So the figure that belongs in place of the question mark should have a white shape with six sides (a hexagon) surrounding an arrow that has been rotated to point straight up. **Answer choice (E)** is correct.

13. Correct Answer: B

In this number series question, you will look at a series of numbers and see what type of pattern is being employed throughout the series. From left to right, the numbers read, "14, 12, 13, 11, 12, 10, 11, 9, ?". While looking for the pattern, it helps to start by noting how the numbers next to each other relate to one another. So, 12 is 2 less than 14, 13 is 1 more than 12, 11 is 2 less than 13, 12 is 1 more than 11, 10 is 2 less than 12, 11 is 1 more than 10, and 9 is 2 less than 11. Here, an alternating pattern of "minus 2, plus 1" emerges. Following this same pattern, since 9 is 2 less than 11, the next number must be 1 more than 9. **Answer choice (B)** is correct.

14. Correct Answer: E

For this numeric inference question, you must identify the pattern that determines the pairs of numbers in each box and then apply that pattern to the pair of numbers in the final box to find the number that belongs in place of the question mark. The first box contains the numbers 13 and 26, the second box contains the numbers 22 and 44, and the third box contains the number 55 and a question mark. So what relationship do the numbers in each pair share? In the first box, you can see that 26 is the same as $13 + 13$, or 2 times 13. In the second box, 44 is the same as 2 times 22. Since the numbers in the third box must follow the same rule, the number that belongs in place of the question mark must equal twice the number 55. Using the equation $55 \times 2 = 110$, **answer choice (E)** is correct.

15. Correct Answer: C

For this number matrix, you will need to look at the rows of numbers in order to identify the pattern that is being applied to the numbers in each row. In the first row are the numbers 1, 4, and 7. How are these numbers related to one another? In order to get the second number, 3 has been added to the first number, and 3 has been added to the second number in order to get the third number. In other words, adding 3 to a number will get you the next number in the row. In the second row, you have the numbers 33 and 36 followed by a question mark. Again, 3 has been added to the first number to get the second number. The numbers in the third row are 92, 95, and 98, and again, 3 has been added to each number to get the next number. By now, it is clear that the pattern is to add 3 to each number to get the next number in the row. The missing number is the third number in the second row. Using the equation $36 + 3 = 39$, **answer choice (C)** is correct.

16. Correct Answer: D

What is the relationship between the first pair of figures in this figural analogy question? The first figure has two diagonal white lines on the left facing inward toward a pair of diagonal black lines on the right. The second figure shows that a white circle has been placed at the center of the lines, and the black-and-white pattern now alternates among the lines. The second figure shows a diamond-like shape composed of white lines on the left and black lines on the right. Here, it is helpful to look at all of the answer choices to see which one follows the same pattern when applied to the first figure in the second pair. Answers (C) and (E) can be eliminated immediately because they are not the same basic shape as the figure in the second part of the analogy. Among the remaining possible answer choices, the only one that features both alternating black-and-white lines and a white circle in the middle is **answer choice (D)**.

17. Correct Answer: B

Here, you must identify what is happening to each figure in the series in order to determine which figure belongs in place of the question mark. The first figure in the series is a white square. In the second figure, a vertical line has been added bisecting the square. The third figure shows that a short diagonal line has been drawn on the right half of the square starting from the center of the vertical line and ending at the top right corner of the square. In the fourth figure, another short line has been drawn from the center of the vertical line, this time going straight out and ending at the center of the right line of the square. Following this pattern, another line should be added starting at the center of the vertical line and ending at the bottom right corner of the square. The correct response is **answer choice (B)**.

18. Correct Answer: D

How do the pairs of numbers in this numerical inference question relate to one another? The numbers in the first box are 9 and 3. Now, 3 is related to 9 in a few different ways. First, 3 is the same as 9 divided by 3, and second, 3 is 6 less than 9. The numbers in the third box are 33 and 27. 27 is not the solution to 33 divided by 3, but 27 is 6 less than 33. So the shared relationship between box one and box three is that the second number is 6 less than the first number. The second box shows the number 21 followed by a question mark in place of the second number. Applying the relationship to find the number that belongs in place of the question mark, you find that 6 less than 21 is 15. The correct response is **answer choice (D)**.

19. Correct Answer: D

For this antonym question, you must identify the word among the answer choices that means the opposite of "immense". If something is immense, it can be described as huge, gigantic, or extremely large. So here you are looking for a word that describes something very small. "Vast" (choice A) describes something very large or extremely wide, so this answer choice is incorrect. "Frigid" (choice B) refers to something that is extremely cold, which is also incorrect. "Calm" (choice C) describes something that is peaceful and quiet, so this answer choice is incorrect. "Incomplete" (choice E) refers to something that is unfinished or deficient in some way. The correct response is answer choice **(D) "tiny"**, which describes something that is miniscule, petite, or extremely small.

20. Correct Answer: C

This sentence completion question asks you to find the pair of words that best complete the sentence in question. Does it make sense to say, "Everyone saw the fire truck driving down the street because the siren was so quiet"? It does not really make sense that anyone's ability to see something would depend on it being quiet. How about, "Everyone felt the fire truck driving down the street because the siren was so interesting"? This does not make much sense, either, because "interesting" doesn't explain why everyone could feel the fire truck. Should the sentence read, "Everyone ran to the fire truck driving down the street because the siren was so subtle"? Again, this does not make sense in context. Does it make sense to say, "Everyone perceived the fire truck driving down the street because the siren was so capable"? Not really. Answer choices (A), (B), (D), and (E) can all be eliminated. The sentence makes the most sense as, "Everyone heard the fire truck driving down the street because the siren was so shrill." Here, "shrill" describes something that is loud and annoying, which describes why everyone could hear it. **Answer choice (C) is correct.**

21. Correct Answer: B

This sentence arrangement question asks you to organize the words "on", "summer", "your", "have", "fun", and "vacation" into the best possible sentence. Then, you must identify the first letter of the last word of the constructed sentence. The words "have" and "fun" seem to go together, as do the words "summer" and "vacation". So far you have "have fun" and "summer vacation". From this you can construct the sentence, "Have fun on your summer vacation." The first letter of the word "vacation" is "v". The correct answer is **(B) v**.

22. Correct Answer: A

For this arithmetic reasoning question, you must determine what number is twice the difference between nineteen and seven. Here, it helps to write everything out into equations according to the order of operations. To begin, you must find the difference between nineteen and seven. Using the equation $19 - 7$, you arrive at the number 12. Now you need to find a number that is twice as many as twelve. Using the equation 12×2, you get the number 24. The correct answer is **(A) 24**.

23. Correct Answer: A

Here, you must use logic and deductive reasoning to figure out the correct answer from the information presented to you. The question states that Hazel got more ice cream scoops than Kenneth and Zeke but fewer scoops than Lina, and that Pedro didn't get any ice cream. You are then asked to determine what you know for certain based on the information presented. You can immediately eliminate answers (B) and (C) because the question never mentions how many scoops of ice cream Kenneth and Zeke got in relation to one another, nor does it state whether or not Kenneth got any ice cream at all. Answer choice (D) can be eliminated because the question does not say anything about anyone's opinion about ice cream. Answer choice (E) can be eliminated because the question states that Zeke has less ice cream than Hazel who has fewer scoops than Lina. Logically, the only answer choice that you know to definitely be true given the information presented is that Lina got more scoops of ice cream than anyone else mentioned in the question. **Answer choice (A) is correct.**

24. Correct Answer: A

This word matrix presents two rows of three words. The first row contains the words "hop", "hope", and "open". The letters "op" remain the same in all three words. In the second word, a letter has been added onto the first word. In the third word, the first letter of the second word has been dropped and another letter has been added to the end. The second row contains the words "no" and "now". Based on the rule from the first row, we know that the missing word must start with an "o" (the "n" having been dropped) and that a new letter must be added to the end. Among the answer choices, the only word that meets these criteria is **(A) "owl"**.

25. Correct Answer: D

This is a verbal analogy question for which you must identify the relationship between the first pair of words in order to find the missing word in the second pair of words. The first pair of words is "cease" and "stop". These two words have the same meaning and are therefore synonyms. The first word in the second pair of words is "start". Based on the relationship between the first set of words, we are looking for a synonym for "start". A "temper" (choice A) is a tone or an angry mood. To "defeat" (choice B) something is to beat or destroy it. To "repeal" (choice C) something is to take it back. To "approach" (choice E) something is to get closer to it. All of these answer choices can be eliminated because they are not synonyms of the word "start". The correct response is **(D) "commence"**, which means to start.

26. Correct Answer: C

You must determine which word does not belong among the words presented in the answer choices of this verbal classification question. The words here are "intellect" (choice A), "wisdom" (choice B), "ignorance" (choice C), "brilliance" (choice D), and "genius" (choice E). "Intellect" refers to a powerful mind with a great capacity for thought and knowledge. "Wisdom" refers to the possession of a great deal of knowledge and experience. "Brilliance" and "genius" are synonyms of each other and refer to someone or something that displays a great deal of intelligence. So answers (A), (B), (D), and (E) are all related to somebody who is very smart. "Ignorance" carries the opposite meaning of "smart", and is the state of lacking knowledge. **Answer choice (C)** contains the word that does not belong with the others.

27. Correct Answer: D

In this logical selection question, you must determine what is necessary for a novel to exist. Can there be novels without "bindings" (choice A)? Bindings are the parts of paper books that hold all of the pages together. However, books can exist in a digital form, or even on a very long scroll, so answer choice (A) can be eliminated. Can novels exist without "titles" (choice B)? It would be unusual, but it is certainly possible for someone to write an entire book and then choose not to title it. Answer choice (B) is incorrect. Do novels have to have "chapters" (choice C)? Most do, but could a novel exist that had no chapters at all? A novel is essentially the telling of a story, and there are many different ways to tell stories. It is certainly possible for a novel without chapters to exist. Do novels need "computers" (choice E) in order to exist? Novels can be hand-written on paper, typed on a typewriter, or even chiseled into stone. Answer choice (E) is incorrect. The correct response to this logical selection question is **(D) writers**. A novel cannot be written without a writer, so answer choice (D) is correct.

28. Correct Answer: E

The first figure in the first analogous pair is a large pentagon with a small square inside of it. The second figure in the first pair is a large square with a small pentagon inside of it. Here, the large and small shapes are switched in size and position from the first figure to the second. The first figure in the second analogous pair is a large triangle with a small circle inside of it. Going by the rule from the first pair of figures, the second figure should be a large circle with a small triangle inside of it. **Answer choice (E) is correct.**

29. Correct Answer: B

In this pattern matrix question, the first row of figures features a plain white triangle followed by the same triangle with a slightly smaller triangle inside it. In the third figure in the first row, a third, even smaller triangle has been placed at the center and the area between the largest and second-largest triangles has been colored black. The second row of figures features a plain white trapezoid, followed by a question mark. The third figure in the second row is a trapezoid with two increasingly smaller trapezoids at the center. The area between the largest and second-largest trapezoid has been colored black. Based on the pattern in the first row, the missing shape in the second row should be a large white trapezoid with a slightly smaller white trapezoid at its center. **Answer choice (B) is correct.**

30. Correct Answer: A

This figural series question asks you to identify the missing figure in the series by figuring out the rule by which the figures in the series progress. The series begins with a black dot, followed by two black dots connected by a black line. The next figure in the series adds another black dot and two connecting lines, forming a triangle. The following figure is a square comprised of four black dots and four connecting lines. The rule for this series appears to be that one dot and lines connecting all the dots have been added to each figure to create the next figure in the series. If one more dot and connecting line is added to the fourth figure, you should end up with a five-sided shape, a pentagon, comprised of dots and connecting lines. **Answer choice (A)** is correct.

31. Correct Answer: E

Here, you must find the missing number by figuring out the rule that governs all the numbers in this series. The given numbers are 2, 6, 14, 30, and 62. So how are the numbers in this series related? The number 6 is the same as 2×3, $(2 \times 2) + 2$, $2 + 2 + 2$, or $2 + 4$. The number 14 is the same as $(6 \times 2) + 2$ or $6 + 6 + 2$. The number 30 is the same as $(14 \times 2) + 2$ or $14 + 14 + 2$. By now, a pattern is emerging among all of the numbers in the series. Lastly, the number 62 is the same as $(30 \times 2) + 2$. The pattern appears to be that the next number in the series is twice the previous number plus two. By using the equation $(62 \times 2) + 2$, you can identify the correct answer as **(E) 126**.

32. Correct Answer: E

Here, we need to determine the pattern between the numbers in each box in this numeric inference question. In the first box, you see the numbers 10, 35, and 30. The numbers in the third box are 22, 47, and 42. Comparing both sets of numbers to find a common rule determining each number, you can see that the second number in each box is 25 more than the first number, and the third number in each box is 5 less than the second number. The second box shows 16, ?, and 36. Going by the rule governing boxes one and three, the missing number from the second box must be 25 more than 16 and 5 more than 36. Using the equation $16 + 25 = 41$, the correct answer is **(E) 41**.

33. **Correct Answer: D**

Take a look at the first row of numbers in this number matrix. The first number is 80, followed by 36, and then 14. The relationship between these numbers appears to be that you divide one of the numbers by 2 and then subtract 4 to get the next number in the row (80 ÷ 2 = 40 and 40 – 4 = 36; 36 ÷ 2 = 18 and 18 – 4 = 14. This same rule governs the numbers in the second row, featuring the numbers 40, 16, and 4. To find the missing number in the third row, you can use the equation (60 ÷ 2) – 4 to identify **(D) 26** as the correct answer.

34. **Correct Answer: C**

Here, we are looking for the word presented in the answer choices that has the opposite meaning of the word "feeble". To be feeble is to be weak or delicate. "Weak" (choice A) is a synonym of feeble, so this answer choice is incorrect. "Tempting" (choice B) refers to something that is enticing or that draws you near. Answer choice (B) is also incorrect. If somebody is "lazy" (choice D), they are sluggish and do not put much effort into things. If you are feeling "anxious" (choice E), you are filled with mental or emotional fear or distress. Answers (D) and (E) are both incorrect. The correct response is **(C) "sturdy"**, meaning "strong" or "hardy", which is the opposite of "feeble".

35. **Correct Answer: D**

The figures in this pattern matrix go together in a certain way. In the first row, the first figure is a straight horizontal line. In the second figure, two black dots have been added above and below the line so that it looks like a division symbol. In the third figure, the line has been rotated 90 degrees so that the line is vertical and the dots are to the right and left of the line. In the second row, the first figure is a plain white circle. The third figure in this row shows the circle with two black dots to the right and left. Assuming that the figures in the second row follow the same rule as the figures in the first row, the circle with the black dots must have been rotated 90 degrees. The missing figure in the second row must therefore be a white circle with a black dot directly above and below it. The correct response is **answer choice (D)**.

36. Correct Answer: A

In this series, there is a pattern consisting of two numbers and a letter. There are also patterns among the numbers and letters separately. You are looking to identify the tenth figure in the series, which will be a number. The pattern affecting the letters seems to be that they are appearing in backwards alphabetical order. The numbers in the series seem to be increasing by 1, starting from the number 3. Looking at all the figures in the series, you can see that every third number is replaced by a letter (3, 4, Z, 6, 7, Y, etc.). The value of the number following each letter is always two more than the number before each letter. The last two figures given in the series are the number 10 followed by the letter X. Following the pattern, the next number in the series should be two more than 10. Answer choice **(A) 12** is correct.

37. Correct Answer: D

While deciding which pair of words best completes the sentence in question, it is important to pay special attention to how the words in each pair relate to each other in the sentence. Words like "although", "nevertheless", and "except" negate whatever comes after them in the sentence. In other words, the second half of the sentence should be surprising given the information presented in the first half of the sentence. Is it surprising to say that, "She wanted to eat the corned beef although she was hungry"? It is not surprising that someone who is hungry would want to eat something, so answer choice (A) is incorrect. Does it make sense to say, "She hurried to eat the corned beef nevertheless she was hungry"? How about, "She hustled to eat the corned beef except she was hungry"? Neither of these sentences makes much sense. Answer choices (B) and (C) are incorrect. Would it be surprising to say, "She resolved to eat the corned beef even if she was hungry"? Again, it is not surprising to make sure you eat something if you are hungry. The correct word pair belongs to **answer choice (D)**, which produces the sentence: "She refused to eat the corned beef although she was hungry."

38. Correct Answer: A

This number matrix features pairs of numbers across the rows. In order to identify the correct answer choice, you must figure out the relationship between the numbers in each pair as they relate to each other pair. The numbers in the top row of the matrix are: "17, 17", "20, 14", and "23, 11". A quick look will show that there does not seem to be a pattern among the pairs themselves, as 17 is 0 less than 17, 14 is 6 less than 20, and 11 is 12 less than 23. The next step is to look at how the first number of each pair relates to the first number of each other pair. Here, 20 is 3 more than 17, and 23 is 3 more than 20. The pattern appears to be that the first number of each pair increases by 3. Now look at the last number of each pair. Here, 14 is 3 less than 17, and 11 is 3 less than 14. The pattern for the last number of each pair seems to be that it decreases by 3. Let's see if these patterns hold up for the second row, which reads: "10, 20", "13, 17", and "?". Here, 13 is 3 more than 10 and 17 is 3 less than 20, so the pattern is the same. Going by the same pattern, the numbers that belong in place of the question mark should be 16 and 14. **Answer choice (A)** is correct.

39. Correct Answer: B

Here, we need to determine how the numbers in each box relate to each other in this numeric inference question. The numbers in the first box are 41, 45, and 53. Here, the first things that you can determine about the numbers in the box are that 45 is 4 more than 41 and 53 is 8 more than 45. The numbers in the second box are 74, 78, and 86. The same pattern emerges, with 78 being 4 more than 74 and 86 being 8 more than 78. The given numbers in the last box are 67 followed by 71. Since 71 is 4 more than 67, the next number must be 8 more than 71. The correct answer is **(B) 79**.

40. Correct Answer: C

The first figure in this analogy shows a large black heart-like shape with a small white triangle at the top of the center of the shape. The next figure in the pair is a vertical series of small white shapes consisting of, from top to bottom: white heart, white triangle, white heart, and a white triangle. The first figure in the next analogous pair shows a large white star with a small white circle at the top of the center of the shape. So what should the next figure in the series be? You know the figure should consist of a vertical series of four shapes, so answers (A), (B), and (D) can immediately be eliminated because they each have a series of five shapes. Based on the first pair of figures, you know that the large star will become smaller and become the first and third shapes in the figure. Furthermore, the color of the star should be reversed to black, since the color of the heart in the first figure was reversed to white. The small white circle should be the second and fourth shapes in the vertical series. The correct response is **answer choice (C)** which shows a vertical series consisting of, from top to bottom: black star, white circle, black star, and a white circle.

41. Correct Answer: A

Using your logic skills, we are trying to determine which of the answer choices presents something that is always associated with fruit. Can you think of a fruit that doesn't have a pit? A pit is a hard stone-like seed at the center of certain types of fruit. Fruits like cherries and apricots have pits, but bananas and apples do not. Answer choice (B) is incorrect. Can you think of fruits that don't have (C) stems? A stem is a stalk that supports a leaf, flower, or a fruit, but a stem is not usually a part of the fruit itself. Similarly, most plants that grow fruits have (D) leaves, but the leaves are not the fruits themselves. Answers (C) and (D) are incorrect. Can you think of a fruit that doesn't have a rind? A rind is a thick outer covering that protects the flesh of fruits like oranges and watermelons. However, fruits like pears and plums do not have a rind, so answer choice (E) is incorrect. The correct response is **(A) seeds**. All fruits, from strawberries to pineapples to mangoes, have seeds.

42. Correct Answer: A

Here, you must identify the missing figure from this pattern matrix. The first row of figures in the matrix shows a plus-sign-like shape followed by an X-like shape. The third figure in the top row combines the two previous figures to make a new figure. In the second row of the matrix, the first figure is an upright equilateral triangle and the last figure is a six-pointed star that seems to be comprised of one upright equilateral triangle and one downward-pointing equilateral triangle. Based on the pattern from the first row, the third figure must be comprised of the two figures preceding it. This means that the second figure in the second row must be a downward-pointing equilateral triangle. **Answer choice (A) is** correct.

43. Correct Answer: C

The numbers in this series are 2, 2, 4, 12, and 48. So what number comes next in the series? Looking at the numbers as they progress, you can see that 2 is 0 more than 2, 4 is 2 more than 2, 12 is 8 more than 4, and 48 is 36 more than 12. So far, that's not much of a pattern, so you should try looking at the numbers in a different way. Looking at the numbers again, you can see that 2 is 2 times 1, 4 is 2 times 2, 12 is 4 times 3, and 48 is 12 times 4. Now a pattern emerges, which appears to be that each number in the series is multiplied by a number that increases by 1, so that the first number is multiplied by 1, the next number by 2, and so on. The next number in the series must therefore be the product of 48 times 5. The correct response is **(C) 240**.

44. Correct Answer: B

This is another question that asks you to arrange a set of words into the best possible sentence. The words presented in the box are "the", "while", "hot", "eat", "it's", and "soup". It makes sense to pair "the" with "soup", since "soup" is the only noun among the set of words. Next, you can group together the words "while", "it's", and "hot" to form a phrase that makes sense. This leaves you with the word "eat", which can logically be placed before "the soup" in the sentence. Now you can construct a sentence out of the pieces that go together which reads: "Eat the soup while it's hot." Next, the question asks you to identify the beginning letter of the first word in the sentence. Since the first word of the sentence is "eat", **answer choice (B)** is correct.

45. Correct Answer: E

For this arithmetic reasoning question, it is helpful to construct a simple algebraic equation to help solve the problem. The question states that there are 16 elephants and bears total at the zoo. It further states that there are 3 times as many elephants as bears at the zoo. So how many bears are at the zoo? Well, you know that the number of elephants is exactly 3 times the amount of bears, which can be written as 3 times b, or 3b. If you add the number of elephants to the number of bears, b, you should get the number 16. This can be written as the equation $3b + b = 16$. Now, 3 times b plus b is the same as 4 times b, which can be written in the equation as $4b = 16$. In order to figure out what number b is, you can divide both sides of the equation by 4, leaving you with $b = 4$. You can check your work by replacing the letter b with the number 4 in the original equation, so that $(3 \times 4) + 4 = 16$. **Answer choice (E)** is correct.

46. Correct Answer: D

Here is another inference question. The question states that Nicole went to the mall on Tuesday and Thursday, Sheryl went to the mall every day of the week but Monday, Friday, and Saturday, and Suzanne never went to the mall on the same day as either Nicole or Sheryl. So what do you know for certain? Looking at the answers, answer choice (C) can be eliminated immediately because the question does not tell you anything about anybody's attitude or preference about going to the mall. Answer choice (A) can be eliminated because the question states that Nicole went to the mall on Tuesday and Thursday, but makes no mention of whether or not she went to the mall on Monday. We know for certain that Sheryl went to the mall on Tuesday, Wednesday, Thursday, and Sunday, and we know that Suzanne never went to the mall on the same day as Sheryl, so answer choice (B), "Suzanne went to the mall on Wednesday," can be eliminated. The question directly states that Sheryl did not go to the mall on Friday, so answer choice (E) can be eliminated. Based on the given information, the one piece of information in the answer choices that we know to be true is that both Sheryl and Nicole went to the mall on Tuesday and Thursday. **Answer choice (D)** is correct.

47. Correct Answer: D

The figures in this series progress according to certain rules which must be identified in order to determine which figure belongs in place of the question mark. The first figure in the series is a square with a black background with a small white square in its upper right corner. In the next figure, it appears that the bottom line of the small square has moved 45 degrees clockwise, increasing the area of the smaller internal shape. Additionally, you can see that the colors of the large shape and the internal shape have been switched, so that the large square is now white, and the smaller internal shape is black. The next figure switches the colors again, but the bottom line of the smaller shape has again moved 45 degrees clockwise. In the next figure, the color-switching pattern continues and the line again moves 45 degrees clockwise. Following this pattern, the final figure in the series should be a larger white square with a small black square in the upper left corner. **Answer choice (D)** is correct.

48. Correct Answer: D

This numeric inference question asks you to find the missing number from the pair of numbers in the third box. To do so, you must figure out how the numbers in the first two boxes relate to one another. The first box contains the number 60 followed by the number 20. The second contains the numbers 30 and 10. Looking at both boxes, you can see that the second number in each pair is one-third of the first number. In other words, the first number in each box is 3 times the second number. The third box reads, "?, 12." In order to find the number that belongs in place of the question mark, you must multiply the second number, 12, by 3. Using the equation 12×3, you can identify **(D) 36** as the correct response.

49. Correct Answer: B

Here we are looking for the word in the answer choices that is the antonym of the word "hasty". To be hasty is to be speedy or quick. Answer choice (A) can be eliminated immediately because "quick" is a synonym, not an antonym, of the word "hasty". If a person is "wasteful" (choice C), he or she is a person who consumes more than his or her fair share. "Wasteful" is not an antonym of "hasty", so answer choice (C) is incorrect. To be "tardy" (choice D) is to be late for something. This may seem like a good answer choice, but is "tardy" truly an antonym of "hasty"? If a speedy person would likely arrive early to an appointment, a slow person would be tardy to that same appointment. Here you can see that you are really looking for a word that has the same meaning as the word "slow", where "tardy" is the consequence of being the opposite of "hasty". Answer choice (D) is also incorrect. To be "content" (choice E) is to be satisfied or happy with the status quo. This is not an antonym of "hasty", so answer choice (E) is incorrect. The correct response is **(B) sluggish**. A sluggish person is someone who moves very slowly, which has the opposite meaning to the word "hasty".

50. Correct Answer: B

The first pair in this figural analogy shows a pentagon with five short lines coming out from each of its points followed by a pentagon with lines starting at its corners and meeting at the center of the shape. Here, it appears as though the lines coming out from the corners have been folded inward so that they point toward each other. The next analogous pair shows a triangle with lines starting at its corners and meeting at the center. In order to have the same relationship as the figures in the first analogous pair, the second figure in the second pair must be a triangle with lines coming out of its corners. **Answer choice (B) is correct.**

51. Correct Answer: C

This number series question is a little bit tricky. You are presented with a series of numbers: 11, 12, 14, 17, 23, 35, and 59. You must figure out which number in the answer choices comes after the number 59. Looking at the numbers in relation to one another, you can see that 12 is 1 more than 11, 14 is 2 more than 12, 17 is 3 more than 14, 23 is 6 more than 17, 35 is 12 more than 23, and 59 is 24 more than 35. At first, the pattern appears to be that a number increasing by 1 is added to each number to get the next number in the series, but this pattern ceases to work once you get to the number 23. Once you get to the number 17, it appears as though a number (starting with the number 3) is multiplied by 2 and then added to each number to get the next number in the series. So what pattern can connect the first half of the series with the second half? Here, it may help to take a closer look at the numerical differences between all the numbers. In order, beginning with the difference between 11 and 12 and ending with the difference between 35 and 59, we get the numbers 1, 2, 3, 6, 12, and 24. So how are these numbers related? The pattern that emerges is that the number added to each number in the series is the sum of all the previous differences in the series. In other words, to get the number 3, you add 1 and 2 together. To get the number 6, you add the previous differences (3, 2, and 1) together, and so on. Based on this rule, in order to find the next number in the series, you must find the sum of all previous numbers added to each number in the series. If you add together 1, 2, 3, 6, 12, and 24, you get the number 48. The next number in the series must be 48 more than the number 59. Since 48 + 59 = 107, **answer choice (C)** is correct.

52. Correct Answer: B

The first row of this pattern matrix features a black dot with a vertical black line above it, followed by the same figure with an added horizontal black line to the left of the dot. The third figure in the first row of the matrix is a mirror image of the second figure, so that the lines are pointing vertically down and horizontally to the right. The second row of the matrix features a black dot with a horizontal white rectangle above it, followed by the same black dot with the rectangle extended vertically down the left side of the black dot. Following the pattern from above, the next figure in the series should be a mirror image of the second figure, with the black dot sitting inside a white corner-like shape that extends vertically on the right and horizontally across the bottom of the dot. The correct response is **answer choice (B)**.

53. ## Correct Answer: E

There are a couple of different rules that govern the number pairs in this number matrix, but there is only one that relates the top row of numbers to the bottom row. The top row of the matrix reads: "3, 4", "7, 8", and "15, 16". The bottom row of the matrix reads: "6, 8", "14, 16", and "?". Now, look at the pairs of numbers vertically as a series of columns. The columns read, from left to right: "3, 4" and "6, 8", "7, 8" and "14, 16" and "15, 16" and "?". Now a clear relationship between the top row of numbers and the bottom row of numbers appears. To get the numbers in the bottom pairs, you must multiply the numbers in each pair on the top row by 2, so that 3 becomes 6, 4 becomes 8, and so on. Applying this rule to the last column, you must multiply 15 by 2 to get the first number and multiply 16 by 2 to get the second number in the missing pair. The correct response is **(E) 30, 32**.

54. ## Correct Answer: A

Which of the answer choices provides the best pair of words to complete the sentence? The best way to identify the answer to this question is to plug in the words from each of the answer choices. Does it make sense to say, "Cooking was simple for him, so he decided to become a father"? Being a father doesn't really have anything to do with cooking being simple, so answer choice (B) is incorrect. Can you say, "Cooking was surprising for him, so he decided to become a cook"? This sentence is vague, and it doesn't really make sense to say that someone became a cook because they found cooking to be surprising. Answer choice (C) is incorrect. What about, "Cooking was haphazard for him, so he decided to become a restaurant owner"? If something is "haphazard" it is disorganized or careless, which would not be a very good way for a restaurant owner to cook. Answer choice (D) is incorrect. Does it make sense to say that cooking was straightforward for him so he decided to become a fireman? Not really. Answer choice (E) is also incorrect. The correct sentence should read, "Cooking was effortless for him, so he decided to become a chef." If cooking is easy for him, it makes sense that he became a chef. **Answer choice (A) is correct.**

55. Correct Answer: A

This is another verbal analogy question. The first pair of words presented in the question are "avoid" and "approach". To avoid something is to stay away from it. To approach something is to get closer to it. These words carry the opposite meaning of one another, meaning they are antonyms. The first word in the second pair presented in the question is "destroy". The second word in the pair must be an antonym of the word "destroy", meaning to break, ruin, or render something useless. To "suspend" (choice B) something is to hang something up high or to postpone something. To "hoist" (choice C) something is to lift it off the ground. Neither of these definitions means the opposite of "destroy", so answer choices (B) and (C) are incorrect. If something "fades" (choice D), it loses its color or vigor. This word is closer to being a synonym to the word "destroy" than an antonym. Answer choice (D) is incorrect. A "tower" (choice E) is a tall structure. If you tower over everyone else, it means that you are very tall. Tower is not an antonym of the word "destroy", so this answer choice is incorrect. The correct answer is **(A) "build"**, which means to construct or strengthen something; the opposite of destruction.

56. Correct Answer: E

The first image in this figural analogy is a figure made up of two white triangles and one black triangle connected at the center in a sort of flower pattern. Here, the triangle on the bottom left is black. The next image is the same figure, but now the triangle on the bottom right is black. There are two rules that could govern this pair of figures. The first is that the second image could be a mirror image of the first figure. The second possible rule is that the color black is migrating counterclockwise around the figure. The first figure in the second pair shows five ovals connected at the center in a star or flower-like pattern. In this case, the oval on the top right is black and the rest are white. Based on the first set of figures you are looking for a figure that either shows the mirror image of the same figure in which the oval on the top left is black, or in which the color black migrates counterclockwise so that the top oval is black. Looking at the answer choices, only one of those potential figures is present. **Answer choice (E)** shows a figure in which the color black has migrated counterclockwise.

57. Correct Answer: D

The numbers in this series are 48, 50, 45, 47, 42, 44, ?, and 41. Looking at the differences between the numbers, you can see that 50 is 2 more than 48, 45 is 5 less than 50, 47 is 2 more than 45, 42 is 5 less than 47, and 44 is 2 more than 42. The pattern appears to be that you alternately add 2 or subtract 5 to get each number in the series. Since 44 is 2 more than the number preceding it, the next number must be 5 less. The correct response is **(D) 39.**

58. Correct Answer: A

What is the best possible way to arrange the words "storm", "found", "the", "during", "refuge", and "he" into a sentence? The word "found" most likely goes with the word "he", forming the phrase "he found". The words "the" and "storm" most likely go together as well. The word "refuge" means "shelter" or "a place safe from danger", which is a logical thing for someone to seek if there is a storm. This brings us to the sentence, "He found refuge during the storm." The question now asks you to identify the first letter of the first word of the sentence. The correct response is **(A) h**.

59. Correct Answer: E

This number matrix contains four rows of three numbers each. So what rule determines the numbers in the matrix? The numbers in the first row are 21, 22, and 24. Looking at the differences between the numbers across the row, you can see that 22 is 1 more than 21 and 24 is 2 more than 22. The numbers in the second row are 27, 34, and 48. Across the row, you can see that 34 is 7 more than 27 and 48 is 14 more than 34. The numbers in the third row are 31, 42, and 64. Here, 42 is 11 more than 31 and 64 is 22 more than 42. Now a pattern has emerged, whereby the third number in each row is determined by adding twice the difference between the first and second numbers in the row. The numbers in the fourth row are 28 and 36, followed by a question mark. Following the pattern, since the difference between 28 and 36 is 8, the next number must be found by using the equation $36 + (8 \times 2)$ or $36 + 16$. The correct answer is **(E) 52**.

60. Correct Answer: C

Here is another figural series question. The first figure in this series is a large white square with a small black dot in the upper right corner. The next figure is a large white circle with a small black arrow pointing straight downward. The third figure is the same square from the first figure with the black dot moved to the bottom right corner. The fourth figure shows the circle from the second figure with the arrow rotated 90 degrees clockwise so that it is pointing to the left. So what patterns govern this group of shapes? Both the dot and the arrow appear to be moving clockwise around the shapes. Since the last figure we are shown is a circle, the next figure must be a square. Since the black dot was in the bottom right corner of the last square, the next square should show that the dot has again moved clockwise so that it is at the bottom left corner of the figure. **Answer choice (C)** is correct.

61. Correct Answer: A

Which word presented in the answer choices does not belong with the others in this verbal classification question? The given words are "French" (choice A), "Asian" (choice B), "African" (choice C), "European" (choice D), and "Australian" (choice E). All of these are words that describe where a person comes from. So what differentiates them? An Australian person is someone who comes from the country and continent Australia. A European person comes from the continent of Europe. An African person comes from the continent of Africa and an Asian person comes from the continent of Asia. A French person comes from the country of France. All of these words refer to a continent with the exception of the word "French" which only refers to a country. **Answer choice (A)** doesn't belong with the others.

62. Correct Answer: C

The words in this word matrix go together in a certain way. The words in the top row are "tend", "?", and "trend". The word in the second row are "sand", "and", and "stand". In the second row, in order to get the second word, the first letter of the first word has been removed. In order to get the third word in the second row, the letter that was previously removed plus one new letter are added to the beginning of the second word. Assuming that the words in the top row follow the same pattern, the second word can be identified by removing the first letter from the first word. Since the first word in the first row is "tend", the second word must be "end". **Answer choice (C)** is correct.

63. Correct Answer: B

The first figure in this series is a large circle with a small triangle at the center. There is a small black arrow inside the circle pointing to the triangle from the left. The second figure in the series is a large square with a small circle at the center. On top of the circle is a black arrow pointing toward the top of the square. The next shape in the series is a large pentagon with a small square at its center. There is a black arrow inside the square pointing toward the square from the right. The fourth figure in the series is a large star with a small pentagon inside it. Underneath the pentagon is an arrow pointing to the bottom of the star. A couple of patterns emerge when looking at the series as a whole. The large shape from the previous figure always becomes the small shape in the next figure. Additionally, the large shape that appears in each figure is a new shape that hasn't appeared before. The black arrow seems to move around 90 degrees in a clockwise pattern, alternating between pointing toward the small shape or pointing toward the lines of the big shape. Based on this pattern, the missing figure in the series should be a large, previously unseen large shape with a small star inside of it. The black arrow should be pointing toward the small star from the left. **Answer choice (B)** is correct.

64. Correct Answer: E

The words in the first pair of this verbal analogy question are "movable" and "object". An object is usually something that you can move, making it "movable". The first word in the next pair is "navigable". If something is "navigable" then it is able to be guided, navigated, or steered. So what kinds of things are navigable? Can you steer a (A) phone? Phones are movable objects, but they are not able to be steered. Answer choice (A) is incorrect. Can you steer a (B) shoe or a (C) statue? Shoes can be worn, but they cannot be guided. A statue is something that is generally meant to remain in one place for a long time. Neither of these things are things that you can steer. Answers (B) and (C) are incorrect. Can you navigate a (D) ruler? A ruler is used for measuring things, not for navigation. The correct answer is **(E) ship**. A ship can be steered or guided, and is therefore "navigable".

65. Correct Answer: D

This is another number matrix question. The top row of the matrix includes the numbers 3 and 23, with a question mark in place of the second number in the row. The bottom row of the matrix is comprised of the numbers 11, 21, and 31. Looking for patterns across the rows, you can see that the numbers in the top row seem to end in 3 and the numbers on the bottom row all end in 1. But how does the top row relate to the bottom row? The rule that governs the bottom row seems to be that the number 10 is added to each number to get the next number in the row. Since the third number in the top row is 20 more than the first number, it is safe to assume that the second number will be 10 more than the first number and 10 less than the third number. The correct response is **(D) 13**. There is one additional way you can identify 13 as the correct answer to this question. Looking at the numbers as columns, you can see that each number in the bottom row is 8 more than the number above it in the top row. The middle number on the bottom row is 21, and 21 − 8 = 13.

66. Correct Answer: C

For this arithmetic reasoning question, you are told that there is a basket filled with apples and oranges. There are 30 fruits total, and there are half as many apples in the basket as oranges. You are asked to figure out how many oranges are in the basket. So, what two numbers add up to 30, where one of the numbers is twice as much as the other? One helpful trick is to visualize the fruits in 3 equal piles, with one pile of apples, one pile of oranges, and one more pile of oranges. If you divide 30 by the number 3, you end up with the number 10. This would mean that there is one pile of 10 apples, one pile of 10 oranges, and one more pile of 10 oranges. Add the number of oranges in each pile together and you can identify **(C) 20** as the right answer.

67. Correct Answer: B

In this pattern matrix, you need to identify the figure that belongs in place of the question mark in the first row. Here, you should first identify the pattern governing the figures on the bottom row. The bottom row of the matrix features three figures. The first figure is a plain, vertical black line. In the second figure, a horizontal line has been added that starts at the top of the vertical line and extends to the right, forming a right angle. The third figure shows that another vertical line has been added, beginning at the right end of the horizontal line and extending downward, creating a table-like shape. In each figure on the bottom row, a line segment is added. The first figure in the top row is a diagonal line that extends to the right at a 45 degree angle. The third figure in the top row shows three connected line segments forming the top half of a hexagon. Based on the pattern in the bottom row, the second figure should be a diagonal line with another line attached to it at the top and extending out to the right. **Answer choice (B)** is correct.

68. Correct Answer: A

This is an inference question. First, you are told that Hope has more lollipops than Deidra and fewer lollipops than Xander. Second, you are told that Vincent has more lollipops than Alex, and Alex has more lollipops than both Xander and Hope. You can immediately eliminate answer choice (B) because the number of lollipops owned is never mentioned for any individual. Look at the first set of information. If Hope has fewer lollipops than Xander, then it's impossible that she has as many lollipops as Xander. You can eliminate answer choice (E). If Xander has more lollipops than Hope, and if Hope has more lollipops than Deidra, then Xander must have more lollipops than Deidra. You can eliminate answer choice (D), the logical opposite of your conclusion. Applying your logic to the second set of information, if Vincent has more lollipops than Alex, and Alex has more lollipops than Xander, then Vincent must have more lollipops than Xander. You can eliminate answer choice (C) which contradicts your conclusion. The correct answer is **(A) Diedra has the least amount of lollipops**. Both Vincent and Alex have more lollipops than Xander. Xander has more lollipops than Hope, and Hope has more lollipops than Deidra. Thus, it follows that all the individuals have more lollipops than Diedra.

69. **Correct Answer: B**

This is a word/letter matrix question. Look at the first row of words in the box. The words are "Triple, ripple, rip". The beginning letter "t" is removed from the first word and the letter "p" is added to get the second word. Only the first three letters "rip" are kept to get the third word. Using this pattern, you need to find the second word in the second row of this word/letter matrix. In the second row, the first word is "dearer" and the third word is "ear". You need to remove the beginning letter "d" from the first word and add a letter somewhere to "earer". The only word among the answer choices that contains the letters "earer" in order with an additional letter is "earner". Therefore, the missing second word and the correct answer is **(B) earner**.

70. **Correct Answer: C**

This is a verbal classification question. Which one of the words provided is not like the other words? The words given to you are "octagon" (choice A), "hexagon" (choice B), "cube" (choice C), "triangle" (choice D), and "square" (choice E). An octagon, a hexagon, a triangle, and a square are descriptions of geometric shapes that are two-dimensional. These shapes can all be placed on a flat plane. A cube is also a geometric shape, but it can be described as being three-dimensional, or as occupying physical space. Since a cube takes up physical space, it cannot be placed on a flat plane, unlike the remaining answer choices. Thus, the word that is not similar to the others is **(C) cube**.

71. **Correct Answer: C**

This is a logical selection question. Here, you are asked to find what police officers cannot do without when completing their job. Police officers work to protect people and property. Does every police officer need to wear a "uniform" (choice B)? While uniforms help individuals identify police officers, police officers do not have to wear them. For example, undercover police officers do not wear uniforms. Similarly, police officers wear "badges" (choice A) to inform others of their protective role. But officers do not need to wear badges in order to complete their jobs. You can eliminate answer choices (A) and (B). Does every police officer need "sirens" (choice D) on his or her police car? Police car sirens warn other traffic or pedestrians of a situation that requires attention. But, police officers do not always need to alert other people; they can watch and stand guard in public places. "Handcuffs" (choice E) help police officers to restrain suspected criminals. However, police officers have the option of not using any restraining devices when holding suspects. Therefore, answer choice (E) is incorrect. Could a police officer fulfill his or her role without "laws" (choice C)? The answer is no. Police officers protect people and property by enforcing laws. If there were no laws to enforce, then police officers would be deprived of their protective duty. Thus, the correct answer is **(C) laws**.

72. **Correct Answer: A**

How do the numbers in each box relate to one another in this numeric inference question? The numbers in the first box are "81, 9." It seems like the first number is divided by 9 in order to get the second number. In the second box, you have numbers "90, 10." Here, the operation of dividing the first number by 9 to get the second number remains. The first number in the third box is "9". Applying the rule observed in the first two boxes, we need to divide this number by 9 to get the second number. $9 \div 9 = 1$. Thus, **answer choice (A)** is correct.

NAME: _____   DATE: _____

EXAMPLE

1 Ⓐ ⊗ Ⓒ Ⓓ   WRONG
2 ✓Ⓐ Ⓑ Ⓒ Ⓓ   WRONG
3 Ⓐ Ⓑ ◖ Ⓓ   WRONG
4 Ⓐ Ⓑ Ⓒ ●   CORRECT

DIRECTIONS:

- Use a #2 black lead pencil only.
- Do not use ink or colored pencil.
- Completely fill in one oval per question.
- Erase clearly any answer you wish to change.
- Make no stray marks on this answer sheet.

Sample Questions
A. Ⓐ Ⓑ Ⓒ Ⓓ Ⓔ
B. Ⓐ Ⓑ Ⓒ Ⓓ Ⓔ
C. Ⓐ Ⓑ Ⓒ Ⓓ Ⓔ
D. Ⓐ Ⓑ Ⓒ Ⓓ Ⓔ
E. Ⓐ Ⓑ Ⓒ Ⓓ Ⓔ

1. Ⓐ Ⓑ Ⓒ Ⓓ Ⓔ
2. Ⓐ Ⓑ Ⓒ Ⓓ Ⓔ
3. Ⓐ Ⓑ Ⓒ Ⓓ Ⓔ
4. Ⓐ Ⓑ Ⓒ Ⓓ Ⓔ
5. Ⓐ Ⓑ Ⓒ Ⓓ Ⓔ
6. Ⓐ Ⓑ Ⓒ Ⓓ Ⓔ
7. Ⓐ Ⓑ Ⓒ Ⓓ Ⓔ
8. Ⓐ Ⓑ Ⓒ Ⓓ Ⓔ
9. Ⓐ Ⓑ Ⓒ Ⓓ Ⓔ
10. Ⓐ Ⓑ Ⓒ Ⓓ Ⓔ
11. Ⓐ Ⓑ Ⓒ Ⓓ Ⓔ
12. Ⓐ Ⓑ Ⓒ Ⓓ Ⓔ
13. Ⓐ Ⓑ Ⓒ Ⓓ Ⓔ
14. Ⓐ Ⓑ Ⓒ Ⓓ Ⓔ
15. Ⓐ Ⓑ Ⓒ Ⓓ Ⓔ
16. Ⓐ Ⓑ Ⓒ Ⓓ Ⓔ
17. Ⓐ Ⓑ Ⓒ Ⓓ Ⓔ
18. Ⓐ Ⓑ Ⓒ Ⓓ Ⓔ
19. Ⓐ Ⓑ Ⓒ Ⓓ Ⓔ
20. Ⓐ Ⓑ Ⓒ Ⓓ Ⓔ
21. Ⓐ Ⓑ Ⓒ Ⓓ Ⓔ
22. Ⓐ Ⓑ Ⓒ Ⓓ Ⓔ
23. Ⓐ Ⓑ Ⓒ Ⓓ Ⓔ
24. Ⓐ Ⓑ Ⓒ Ⓓ Ⓔ

25. Ⓐ Ⓑ Ⓒ Ⓓ Ⓔ
26. Ⓐ Ⓑ Ⓒ Ⓓ Ⓔ
27. Ⓐ Ⓑ Ⓒ Ⓓ Ⓔ
28. Ⓐ Ⓑ Ⓒ Ⓓ Ⓔ
29. Ⓐ Ⓑ Ⓒ Ⓓ Ⓔ
30. Ⓐ Ⓑ Ⓒ Ⓓ Ⓔ
31. Ⓐ Ⓑ Ⓒ Ⓓ Ⓔ
32. Ⓐ Ⓑ Ⓒ Ⓓ Ⓔ
33. Ⓐ Ⓑ Ⓒ Ⓓ Ⓔ
34. Ⓐ Ⓑ Ⓒ Ⓓ Ⓔ
35. Ⓐ Ⓑ Ⓒ Ⓓ Ⓔ
36. Ⓐ Ⓑ Ⓒ Ⓓ Ⓔ
37. Ⓐ Ⓑ Ⓒ Ⓓ Ⓔ
38. Ⓐ Ⓑ Ⓒ Ⓓ Ⓔ
39. Ⓐ Ⓑ Ⓒ Ⓓ Ⓔ
40. Ⓐ Ⓑ Ⓒ Ⓓ Ⓔ
41. Ⓐ Ⓑ Ⓒ Ⓓ Ⓔ
42. Ⓐ Ⓑ Ⓒ Ⓓ Ⓔ
43. Ⓐ Ⓑ Ⓒ Ⓓ Ⓔ
44. Ⓐ Ⓑ Ⓒ Ⓓ Ⓔ
45. Ⓐ Ⓑ Ⓒ Ⓓ Ⓔ
46. Ⓐ Ⓑ Ⓒ Ⓓ Ⓔ
47. Ⓐ Ⓑ Ⓒ Ⓓ Ⓔ
48. Ⓐ Ⓑ Ⓒ Ⓓ Ⓔ

49. Ⓐ Ⓑ Ⓒ Ⓓ Ⓔ
50. Ⓐ Ⓑ Ⓒ Ⓓ Ⓔ
51. Ⓐ Ⓑ Ⓒ Ⓓ Ⓔ
52. Ⓐ Ⓑ Ⓒ Ⓓ Ⓔ
53. Ⓐ Ⓑ Ⓒ Ⓓ Ⓔ
54. Ⓐ Ⓑ Ⓒ Ⓓ Ⓔ
55. Ⓐ Ⓑ Ⓒ Ⓓ Ⓔ
56. Ⓐ Ⓑ Ⓒ Ⓓ Ⓔ
57. Ⓐ Ⓑ Ⓒ Ⓓ Ⓔ
58. Ⓐ Ⓑ Ⓒ Ⓓ Ⓔ
59. Ⓐ Ⓑ Ⓒ Ⓓ Ⓔ
60. Ⓐ Ⓑ Ⓒ Ⓓ Ⓔ
61. Ⓐ Ⓑ Ⓒ Ⓓ Ⓔ
62. Ⓐ Ⓑ Ⓒ Ⓓ Ⓔ
63. Ⓐ Ⓑ Ⓒ Ⓓ Ⓔ
64. Ⓐ Ⓑ Ⓒ Ⓓ Ⓔ
65. Ⓐ Ⓑ Ⓒ Ⓓ Ⓔ
66. Ⓐ Ⓑ Ⓒ Ⓓ Ⓔ
67. Ⓐ Ⓑ Ⓒ Ⓓ Ⓔ
68. Ⓐ Ⓑ Ⓒ Ⓓ Ⓔ
69. Ⓐ Ⓑ Ⓒ Ⓓ Ⓔ
70. Ⓐ Ⓑ Ⓒ Ⓓ Ⓔ
71. Ⓐ Ⓑ Ⓒ Ⓓ Ⓔ
72. Ⓐ Ⓑ Ⓒ Ⓓ Ⓔ